The Money Matrix

THE MONEY MATRIX

First published in 2022 by Dragonfly Publications.

Copyright © Nicole Bayliss, 2022

All rights reserved. The moral rights of the author have been asserted under *Copyright Amendment (Moral Rights) Act 2000*.

Except as permitted under the Australian *Copyright Act 1968* (for example, a fair dealing for the purposes of study, research, criticism or review), no part of this book may be reproduced, stored in a retrieval system, communicated or transmitted in any form or by any means without prior written permission.

ISBN: 978-0-6452936-2-3

Printed by Ingram Spark.
Cover Design and Layout: Ben Crompton Design

For information on ordering further copies of the book or to contact the author please visit nicolebayliss.com.au

10 9 8 7 6 5 4 3 2 1

A catalogue record for this book is available from the National Library of Australia

The Money Matrix

12 Truths To Heal Your Relationship with Money and Create Financial Abundance

Nicole Bayliss

This book is dedicated to all those who have taught me lessons about money - my loved ones as well as my enemies.

Contents

Introduction	11
It's okay to talk about money	17
Whatever you believe about money you create	25
You must recognise your limiting beliefs about money	35
Money comes from the Source	47
Abundance is your Divine birthright	55
You are worthy of wealth	63
You must recognise your self-sabotaging behaviours	71
You can heal from past mistakes, loss and debt	83
You must create wealth-affirming behaviours	91

You can have a healthy relationship with money	103
Be prepared for miracles and challenges	113
There are 4 keys to staying on the money matrix	123
Conclusion	135
A Simple Meditation Practice	139
About the Author	145

Introduction

This is a book that I have been wanting to write for some time, because financial disempowerment has affected many people in the world, creating poverty, inequality and a lack of opportunity.

Financial freedom is a topic that comes up over and over again for my clients. We are all here to live our best lives, but how can we do that if we don't have enough money to do the things we need to do and want to do, and own the things we need to enjoy life?

An inability to manifest money can keep us trapped. Trapped in jobs we don't want to be in, trapped in relationships or situations that may not be good for us, and unable to access the goods and services that we require to be well and happy. This is the matrix of scarcity and limitation, but you do not have to stay trapped in it.

It all comes down to your relationship with money, and this relationship is primarily ancestral. For millennia, money has been enjoyed by the few, while many have had so little. Past experiences of poverty and hardship create and reinforce beliefs of poverty and hardship which get handed down from generation to generation. You no longer need to live this way.

What I have come to know through my own life experience and through those of my clients, is that financial abundance is possible, and it's not as difficult as your conditioned mind would have you believe.

It is not your past or your current circumstances that are preventing you from having an abundant flow of money; it is your past and current relationship with money that is preventing you from having an abundant flow of money.

You have the power to create wealth. We all do. Abundance is your Divine right, even if you haven't been brought up to believe this. It is your Divine right even if you were born into a family that struggled financially, even if you are currently struggling financially and even if you never finished your education.

The purpose of this book is to release you from all that is preventing you from having the money you need and want, and to take you out of the matrix of scarcity and limitation and into a matrix of abundance and unlimitedness. Throughout this book, I will be referring to this matrix as the money matrix.

You are worthy of living your best life! You are worthy of being here and enjoying the infinite abundance that the earth has to offer. In this book, we are going to be exploring and clearing the causes of financial struggle on the spiritual, psychological and practical levels. I will be teaching you some very important

Universal Laws and aligning you to the truth of who you really are and the financial flow that you deserve.

So if you are ready to open your heart and mind and let go of old ideas, beliefs and behaviours that prevent you from enjoying financial freedom, I'd love you to join me on this journey. Are you ready? Let's begin!

You deserve to live your best life.

You deserve to be abundant.

Love and light,

Truth Number 1

It's okay to talk about money

It's Okay to Talk About Money

I'd like to take you back with me to the year 1970. That day a fellow Year 2 classmate walked to the front of the class for "News" and announced excitedly that her dad had just been given a pay rise and he was now earning $100 a week (well this was 1970!). The whole class was impressed. So that evening at the family dinner table, I excitedly told my mother and father about my classmate's father getting a pay rise and asked "How much do you earn a week Daddy?" Well you could have heard a pin drop.

"Nicky," said my mother in an icy tone *"it is very rude to talk about money and you NEVER ask anyone what they earn."*

I blushed in shame. This message was heard loud and clear and never again did I bring up the subject. I took this message with me well into my adulthood, and would squirm whenever anyone mentioned money. When negotiating a salary, I would leave it to my employer to name the terms. I would never ask for more than what they offered. Later on in life as an artist, people would offer to buy my paintings, and I would feel myself contract with awkwardness. Talking about money and negotiating a price was not in my comfort zone. I would sabotage these opportunities rather than talk about money.

No communication ever happened in my family around money unless it was to express the lack of it, and therefore there was never any healing opportunity for me around my relationship with money.

When I began my business as a coach and healer, and needed to charge for my services, my dysfunctional relationship with money became glaringly obvious to me. By this stage of my life, however, I knew that I had a problem and that I needed to investigate it. The time had come for me to take responsibility for what

I was creating, or NOT creating to be more precise. I realised I had never felt empowered when it came to money, I found it difficult to talk about and I held a lot of shame because of my own sense of financial disempowerment. Well I've clearly gotten over this, because here I am writing a book about money!

I've since come to know that many people feel:

- embarrassed talking about money

- disempowered when it comes to money

- a sense of shame around money

So why do so many of us feel embarrassed, disempowered and ashamed when it comes to the subject of money? Because the subject is loaded!

Not only with the energy of your current financial reality, but the old stories, fears, disappointments and failures. And loaded with the beliefs we took on from our families, and behind those beliefs the ancestral traumas of struggle and scarcity.

If you feel uncomfortable talking about money, disempowered when it comes to money or a sense of shame around money, it is not your fault. You haven't deliberately created this.

Take a deep and cleansing breath and say:

I acknowledge I've found it difficult to talk about money.

I acknowledge the disempowerment I feel around money.

I acknowledge the shame I hold around money.

I am willing to change!

I am willing to release the disempowerment I feel around money.

I am willing to release the shame I hold around money.

I am willing to talk about money.

Now let's talk about money!

Truth Number 2

Whatever you believe about money you create

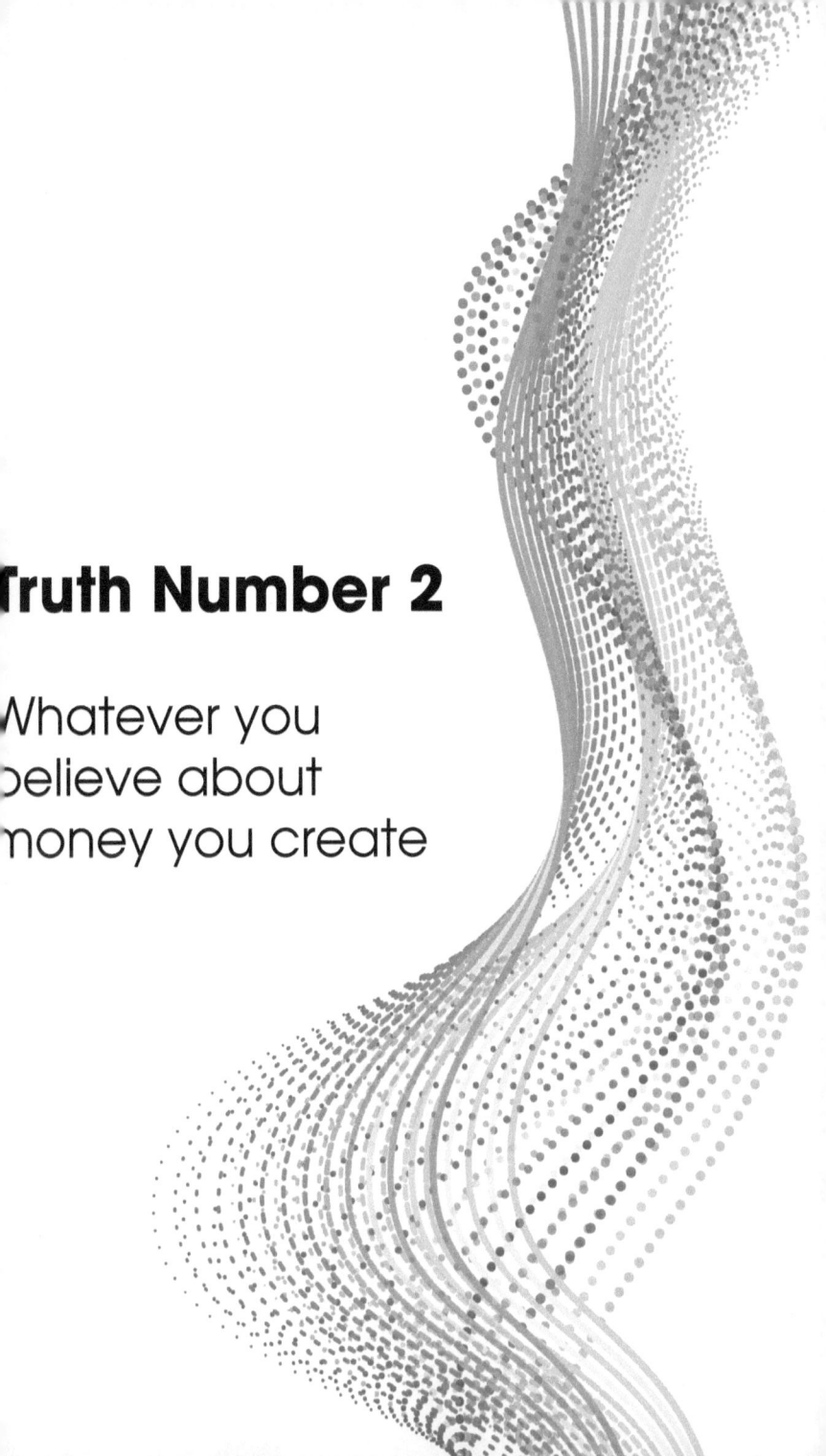

Whatever you believe about money you create

No one deliberately creates financial hardship. Most of our financial troubles stem from our subconscious and even unconscious mind. Many of us hold old programming that keeps us in survival mode. Our ancestors struggled, and so we still struggle. Our "money programming" stems from our family of origin, which goes back further to old ancestral traumas of poverty and hardship.

Money is simply a vehicle of exchange, and it is an effective vehicle of exchange because when we receive money for our goods and services, we can exchange that money for anything we want. And yet, many of us have an uncomfortable relationship with money. Money is not the problem. It never has been. It is neither good nor bad. Onto money we project many beliefs.

The Universal Law of Belief deems that whatever we believe we create, so if you believe that money is hard to come by, you will experience a lack of money. And the created experience of financial hardship then reinforces the belief which then recreates the reality.

What you believe about money will either expand or limit your abundance. When I began to examine my own relationship with money, I realised I was still holding many limiting beliefs which came from my family. Some of them were not spoken beliefs, so I couldn't pinpoint why I would believe what I did, but I realised that these were deeply imprinted in my psyche and had been handed down from previous generations, and were a conglomerate of many old ancestral experiences and traumas.

We also receive messages of scarcity and limitation from the media, educational institutions, governments and even our friends and loved ones. The current reality on our planet is the sum total of everything we, as a mass, believe. And because most of the world is still believing in scarcity and limitation, the created reality just keeps reinforcing our belief in lack and limitation. We see it all around us!

So the beliefs of the mass consciousness create the world reality, and the world reality reinforces the mass beliefs, which then goes on regenerating the world reality. The present reality for most people on earth is a matrix of scarcity and limitation.

But wait!

In this present moment you have the ability to break free from this ever-repeating reality. You do not have to live on the matrix of scarcity and limitation any longer.

This Universal Law of Perpetual Transmutation of Energy deems that we have within us the power to change any circumstance.

While most people in the world still believe that they are victims of circumstance, within every one of us is the ability to transcend difficulties, and to transmute negative circumstances into positive ones.

The power is within you to remove yourself from the matrix of scarcity and limitation and break free. You can decide in this present moment that you are going to live in a self-created reality based on abundance and unlimitedness, a matrix where money flows to you easily, where you always have enough money to do the things you want to do and need to do, and to own the things that will enable you to live your best life.

So what's the catch? The catch is that you must be willing to open your mind and let go of old self-limiting beliefs about money and yourself, to actuate the necessary changes and to open yourself to the ancient truths that will set you free.

The Universal Law of Abundance deems that you have within yourself everything to create an abundant life. We all have, no matter what our circumstances. We live in a Universe of infinite abundance, but most of the population of the world right now believes in a world of lack.

If you are willing to commit to the process, declare now:

I no longer wish to live on the matrix of scarcity and limitation.

I am willing to open my mind and let go of my old limiting beliefs about money.

I am willing to let go of old limiting beliefs about myself.

I am open to the truth about money and who I really am.

> *I am willing to change.*

Let us now explore the beliefs that keep you on the matrix of scarcity and limitation.

Truth Number 3

You must recognise your limiting beliefs about money

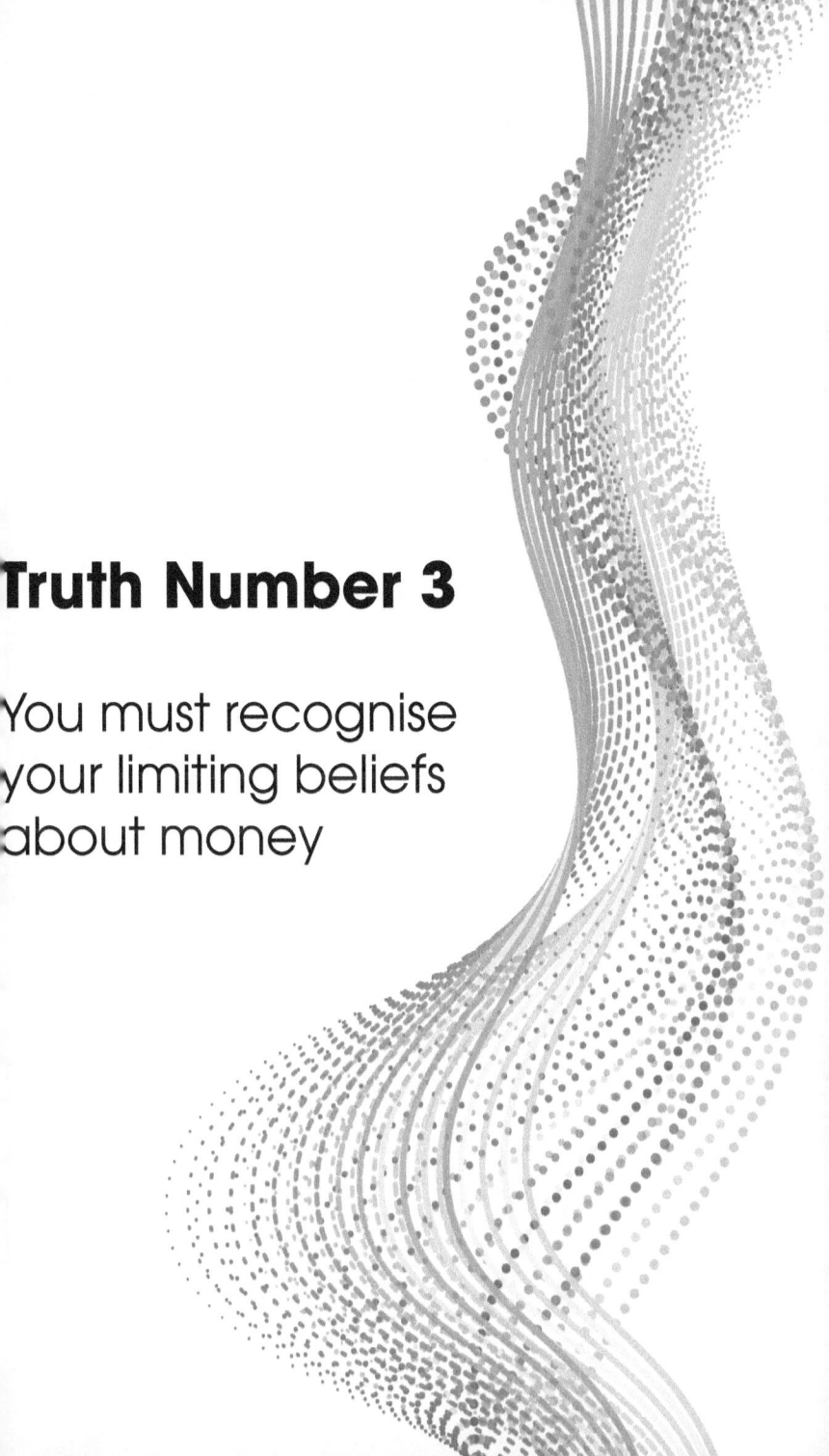

You must recognise your limiting beliefs about money

I'd like you to consider the following beliefs:

- Money doesn't grow on trees
- There is only ever so much to go around
- You have to work very hard to make money
- You cannot do work you love AND make money
- Money is the root of all evil
- It is virtuous to be poor
- Wealthy people are selfish people
- You cannot be spiritual and wealthy
- It's wrong to focus on money
- If you focus on money you don't care about people

- Money isn't important

- It is impolite to talk about money.

Do you relate to any of these beliefs? As I have already shared with you, we inherit these beliefs from our families and their origin lies in the histories of our ancestors. Let's explore each one.

Money doesn't grow on trees - this belief essentially tells us that money is hard to come by. This may have been the experience in your family; it was in mine. The phrase "we can't afford it" was said regularly in my childhood home.

My ancestors were economic refugees like so many who settled in the New World. It really wasn't that long ago that people experienced The Great Depression, the world wars, the Irish Famine, The Highland Clearances in Scotland and extreme poverty in general. Is it any wonder that we are still believing that money is hard to come by? If we are still believing this, then our reality will be a scarcity of money.

There is only ever so much to go around - having "just enough to get by" was the experience for many in the past, and if we are still believing that there will only ever be so much to go around, that is what we will keep creating.

You have to work very hard to make money - over the past few millennia our ancestors were mostly farmers. The harder they toiled, the more likely they were to have enough. Less than two hundred years ago we experienced the industrial revolution, where many people had to work dangerously long hours in appalling conditions to make enough money.

The harder they worked, the more money they would make (even if it was still very little). Based on the "Age of Productivity", this belief is still deeply ingrained in our psyche. And if we are still believing this, we are likely to be working very hard to make our money, and often unable to take time off to enjoy the fruits of our labours.

You cannot do work you love AND make money - I received this message from my parents. They didn't mean to limit me; they were trying to protect me because this had been their experience. For most of the world population until recently, work has meant sacrifice. It has meant doing something that you do not necessarily want to do but have to do, so as to make money.

Many of us do not feel worthy of doing something that we truly love to do and get paid for it. And yet that is what you are really here to do. The Universal Law of Dharma deems that we are here to use our strengths and talents and that when we do, we shall create abundance. If you believe you cannot do work you love and make money, you will likely be in a job that doesn't fulfill you, but you are able to pay the bills.

Money is the root of all evil - there have been many wealthy people in the past who have used money for evil purposes - for power and control over others, to exploit others and resources, and for self-indulgence. People like this exist to this day. From this truth has developed the belief that money is the root of all evil.

Money is neutral. It is neither good nor bad. It is a vehicle of exchange. Money can be used for good purposes or for bad purposes. When we have money, we can be vulnerable to temptation and to misuse money, but it is not the fault of money! When we have money, we also have the option to use it wisely and generously. If you believe that money is evil, you may be repelling money.

It is virtuous to be poor - because money was seen as the root of all evil, of course it was virtuous to be poor! And if we stayed poor, we were out of temptation's way. Vows of poverty were taken in religious orders and to this day, many of us still believe on some level that there is virtue in poverty. If this belief is still active in you, you are likely to be poor. You may feel virtuous, but are you truly happy?

Wealthy people are selfish people - in the past, many wealthy people were selfish people. In the feudal system, the landowners ruled the peasants with little regard for their circumstances. Today, some wealthy people are selfish people and some wealthy people use at least some of their money benevolently. Believing this, we are unlikely to be wealthy.

You cannot be spiritual and wealthy - because wealth has been equated with selfishness, is it any wonder that we believe this? Many religions have taught us that to be spiritual means to sacrifice, so being wealthy cannot equate to being spiritual. This is an interesting concept, given the wealth of the Catholic church, which encouraged this belief. This is another belief that will keep us struggling financially.

It's wrong to focus on money - just as denying money was seen as spiritual and good, focusing on money was seen as selfish and greedy. Whatever we do not put our focus on has no chance to manifest and grow, so if you hold this belief, you are not likely to manifest and grow money.

If you focus on money you don't care about people - those who focus only on money probably don't care about people, but we can focus on money AND also care about people. This belief is closely related to the belief that you cannot be spiritual and wealthy, and it is why many kind and empathic people, especially women and healers, are disempowered financially.

Money isn't important - this belief denies the importance of money and stems from the belief that money is the root of all evil. There are many aspects of abundance - relationships, wellness, things, purpose - as well as money. All are important. Money is the basis of exchange in our current world, so of course it is important! If you believe that money isn't important to you, it won't be, and it will bypass you.

It is impolite to talk about money - because money has been loaded with so many negative experiences and beliefs, it is not surprising that we believe it is impolite or not okay to talk about money. And believing this, we shy away from conversations that could be helpful and opportunities to learn more about money.

We cannot change what we are not aware of. If any of these beliefs are yours, lovingly acknowledge them.

It is time to declare:

I accept that I have been holding limiting beliefs around money.

I am willing to release these beliefs now.

I am willing to know the truth about money.

I am willing to expand into ever greater financial abundance!

And now it is time to know the truth about money.

Truth Number 4

Money comes from the Source

Money comes from the Source

Money comes from the Source of All Things. On an earthly level, it appears that money comes from your job, your business, the government, your investment, your clients, your spouse or from whatever or whomever you receive it. But all of these are just channels through which the Source sends you money. They are NOT the Source!

So what is the Source? It is a loving and supportive matrix of energy that is within and all around you. Some refer to this energy matrix as God. Some prefer other names, such as Universe. The Source is all-loving, all-intelligent and all-knowing. You can choose to be a part of this matrix of energy or not. Acknowledging that there is a Source is imperative if you wish to create abundance easily and without negative consequences.

Choosing to do this alone, in a disconnected way, is the hardest way to manifest money and will not bode well for your future outcomes.

Money is only one part of the whole picture of abundance. As stated in Truth 3, abundance also includes love, relationships, wellness and purpose.

When accessing money through the Source, you can rest assured that the Source will not sacrifice these other areas of abundance so that you can have money. But the disconnected self, the ego, does not have the same ability.

So the Source is the provider of everything, but too often you can become attached to the channel, believing that it is the Source. When you become too attached to a channel or channels through which money comes to you, you close yourself off to the MANY channels that are available to you, because you remain unaware of them.

To receive money from the Source, you must

remain completely open. Money can come to you in ways that you would never have dreamed of, but unless you are open and willing to receive, the opportunities will bypass you. The Source Intelligence is all-powerful and can manifest in unlimited and surprising ways.

When you focus only on the current earthly reality and the limited ways that money currently comes to you, you close yourself off to the unlimited possibilities that are available to you. They are always there.

When you join in the mass belief of negative circumstances such as an economic downturn, a pandemic, a recession, a depression, inflation or unemployment, you allow that reality to take over and disempower you.

When you refuse to identify with these earthly realities, you become the power. You operate from a different matrix to all those still in the reality of mass belief, and you have the ability to transcend scarcity and limitation.

When you open yourself up to ALL the channels of abundance, you will begin to become aware of the unlimitedness. Money may come directly to you in different ways. Ideas and inspirations may come to you, that will lead you to making more money or you may be sent opportunities, helpful people or information that will lead to growing your wealth.

Openness and willingness to receive brings you to the matrix of abundance and unlimitedness - the money matrix - and from this matrix you are able to receive Divinely right abundance.

It is time to declare:

I am a part of the Universal Source.

> *I am open to ALL the channels through which the Source sends me money.*
>
> *I am open to ALL the channels through which the Source sends me ideas and inspiration.*
>
> *I am open to ALL the channels through which the Source sends me opportunities.*
>
> *I am open to ALL the channels of abundance.*

And there is another important truth I wish to share with you.

Truth Number 5

Abundance is your
Divine birthright

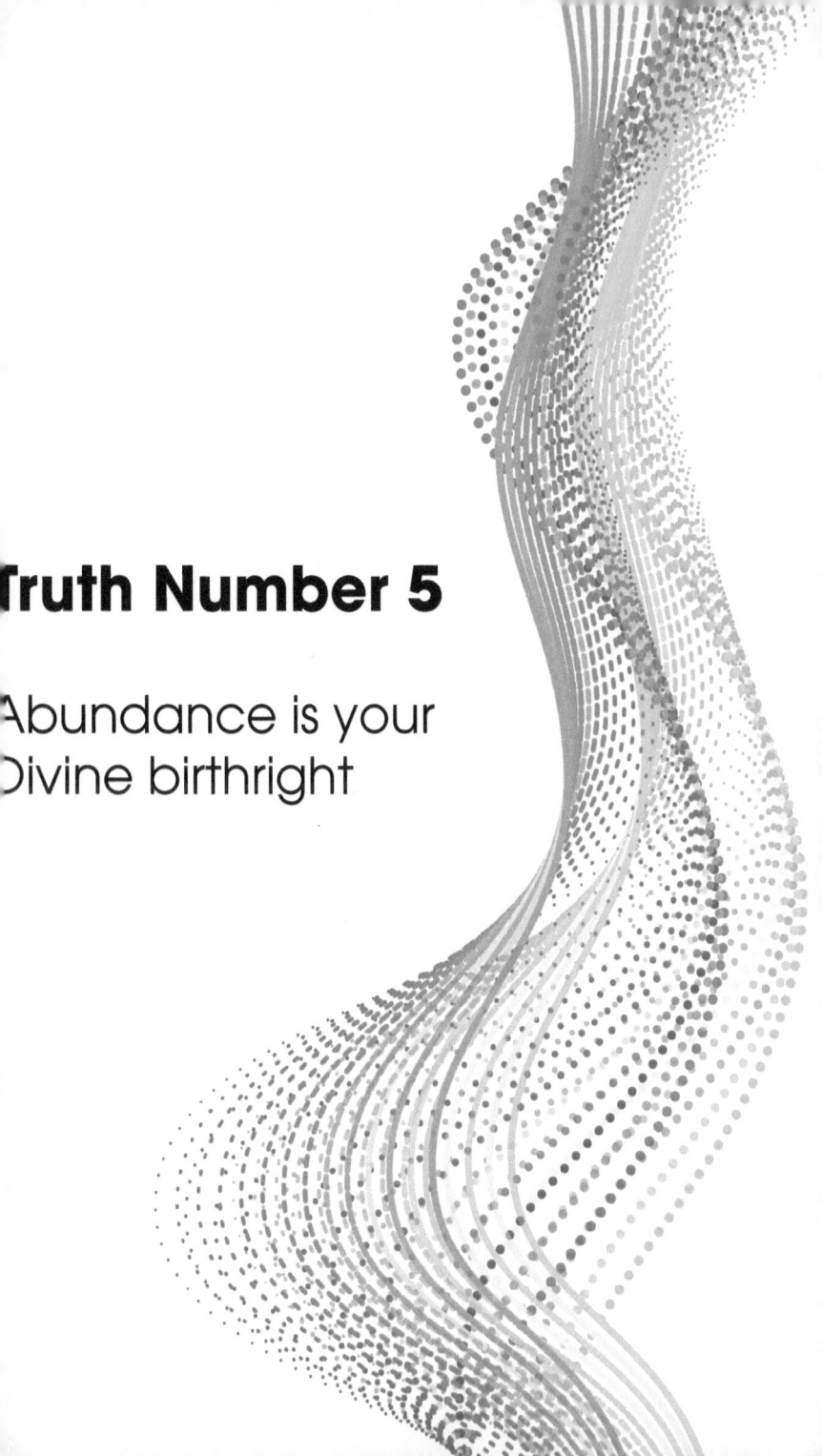

Abundance is your Divine birthright

Abundance is your Divine birthright. This is the premise of the Universal Law of Abundance. You have everything within you to create an earthly paradise. We live in a world of abundance although most people living on the earth at this point in time still believe in a world of scarcity.

The intention for your incarnation was not to struggle, but to thrive. You are born to the Earth and the Earth shall provide, but because most of humanity has lived out of alignment with its true nature for so long, this knowledge has been lost and our connection to Mother Earth has been disturbed.

There has been no better metaphor for this truth than the Biblical story of Adam and Eve. Adam and Eve lived in the Garden of Eden where they enjoyed abundance, but they ignored God's will and gave into temptation. Eve ate from the tree of good and evil and they were cast out of the Garden of Eden, and into a world of scarcity, hardship and struggle. This is the story of mankind!

When our connection to Mother Earth is intact, we will find ourselves "in flow" and receiving Divinely right abundance. And by Divinely right abundance, I mean everything you need to live your best life. This is the Garden of Eden! This is the money matrix!

Abundance includes everything that we need to live our best life - good health, love, connection, meaning, purpose, peace, relaxation and physical things. So while this book is about money, it is imperative that you are aware that money will not solve every problem in life and that there are other aspects of abundance that are just as important as having money.

You are worthy of everything you require to live your best life. You are worthy of everything that is in your highest good. The very fact that you have incarnated on Earth qualifies you to receive all that you require to reach your full potential this lifetime.

When you are grounded to Mother Earth and connected to the Divine Source, you become a co-creator. The energies of both Earth (Yin) and Source (Yang) are each necessary if you are to access your true and full wealth potential. You are here to create Heaven on Earth. You have infinite spiritual power to manifest all that you require for your ultimate earthly experience.

Because of the ancestral imprints of limitation, we have been believing that we are not worthy of such abundance. We have been believing that hardship and struggle is the way that it is. We have believed this because we have been living on that matrix. We are capable of ascending to a new matrix, a matrix where everything flows to us when we need it and away from us when it is no longer required. A matrix where life is not hard; it is easy.

The Universal Law of Least resistance deems that there is a Universal Flow and the flow is downstream. We do not need to swim upstream. We can flow like water flows, and money can flow to us just like water flows. And there is an infinite supply of money. There is no shortage, no blockage in this flow.

It is time to declare:

Abundance is my Divine birthright!

I am worthy of all that I require to live my best life.

I am worthy of everything that is in my highest good.

I am connected to both Heaven and Earth.

There is an infinite supply of money that flows easily to me.

I choose to live on the matrix of abundance and unlimitedness.

I am here to create my Heaven on Earth.

So if abundance is your Divine birthright, you are worthy of it.

Truth Number 6

You are worthy of wealth

You are worthy of wealth

You are worthy of wealth, but on many levels you may not believe it. As I have already stated, behind every limiting belief we have around money is the very real and tragic history of many of our ancestors who experienced scarcity, poverty, hardship and famine.

Most of humanity is not in touch with their true worth. No one has told them and no one has shown them. People do not believe possible what they have not yet experienced.

At the very core of most human beings is the belief that they are not enough. Too many people still believe that they are incapable of creating wealth and do not have what it takes to go beyond their present reality.

The early messages that they received did not encourage them to believe in themselves and their abilities, but the message is here now. You CAN go beyond what you know now. All self-limiting beliefs are transcendable, no matter where they came from.

The limiting beliefs that stem from low self-worth have kept many people trapped and limited in their circumstances. Self-limiting beliefs lead to a lack of self-love and an innate undeservedness that blocks the flow of money. They have kept millions of people unable to go beyond survival mode.

People do not believe possible what they have not yet experienced, but that does not mean that it is impossible. It is possible! The Universal Law of Pure Potential deems that you are pure potential and that you have the ability to expand well beyond what you know yourself and your abilities to be now.

Contemplate the following beliefs:

- I'm not good enough

- I'm not capable

- I'm not worthy or deserving

- I'm not important.

If you relate to any of these beliefs, lovingly acknowledge them. It is not your fault if you believe them. These beliefs would have been imprinted early into your psyche and stem from early traumas, experiences and negative messaging. Let's explore how they block money from flowing to us.

I'm not good enough - the belief that we're not good enough creates the feeling of shame. From this low vibration, we disconnect from our Divine right of abundance. Remember, if you are born to the Earth, the Earth shall provide. There are no other stipulations. You qualify!

I'm not capable - many of us got the message when we were young that we weren't capable of something, which leads us to thinking that we are inferior and not as capable as other people to create wealth. We all have innate capabilities. We are all unique and have different strengths and weaknesses.

When we focus on our strengths, true abundance will follow. The Law of Dharma deems that we have all incarnated with a purpose, and when we align to that purpose, we shall also receive divinely right abundance.

I'm not worthy or deserving - early traumas and negative messages create this belief. But no matter who you are, you are worthy and deserving of abundance.

I'm not important - when we believe we are not important, we will treat ourselves as unimportant and therefore deny ourselves the abundance that is given to us freely from the Universe. Every human being on earth right now is important, including you.

And so it is time to declare:

I have incarnated on Earth and I am therefore good enough!

I am capable of creating perfect wealth.

I am worthy and deserving of perfect wealth.

I am an important soul.

I open myself to the abundance that is given to me freely from the Universe.

Yes, you are worthy of wealth; so it is time to align your actions to your new knowledge and self-worth.

Truth Number 7

You must recognise your self-sabotaging behaviours

You must recognise your self-sabotaging behaviours

Be mindful of your behaviour when it comes to money. You are a spiritual being having a human experience. Changing your beliefs and mindset around money is the first step, but without aligned action it means nothing. As human beings, we must take responsibility for our actions.

The Universal Law of Action requires us to take action that supports and moves us towards what we want, and not away from what we want. When we take aligned action, the Universe takes us seriously and supports us. But if our actions are those that sabotage wealth, no amount of changing beliefs and mindset will put us on the money matrix.

Intention without aligned action is wishful thinking. So as to embody your new beliefs, you must take actions that are aligned with them.

The Universal Law of Karma deems that for every action, there is a reaction. When we choose actions that are in our highest good and the highest good of all, we shall create no negative karma, but should we choose actions that are not in our highest good or not in the highest good of all, bad karma will follow. So there are only ever actions that serve us and actions that do not serve us.

Below is a checklist of behaviours that will sabotage wealth. Be kind and compassionate to yourself as you read through this list, as these are common mistakes that people make. Until we know better, we cannot do better!

Not creating a financial goal or vision -start with the end in mind. Without a financial goal or vision, you have nothing to work towards.

Not knowing your current financial situation - in order to get to your goal or vision, you must know your starting point.

Not planning or budgeting - creating a basic financial plan or budget makes you more conscious of where your money goes and gives you the necessary parameters so as to get ahead.

Not prioritising your spending (wants VS needs) - spending money on your basic needs must come before the non-essentials, for example there is no point in paying for new clothes and entertainment if you haven't paid for your rent, utility bills and food.

Living beyond your current means - this is a form of denial which will eventually catch up with you and ensure that you never get financially abundant.

Getting into debt - there is both good debt (such as a mortgage or a student loan) and bad debt (credit card debt, hire purchase agreements). Once you get yourself into bad debt, it can be difficult to climb out of, as the interest builds. It takes conscious effort to break free of bad debt, so the best way out of bad debt is not to get into bad debt in the first place.

Feeling resentful about paying your way in life - resentment is a toxic emotion and when you resent paying your bills, your taxes or anything else that is necessary for your earthly experience, you will prevent money from flowing back to you. Love will re-establish the flow.

Working on a salary for less than you deserve / Charging for less than you deserve - playing small will keep your financial potential small. The Universe will only ever match what you think you are worthy of.

Working for no pay at all - when you deny yourself, the Universe will also deny you. It is ok if you choose to work on a voluntary basis because you want to make a positive difference in some way, but if you would like or need to earn money, then seek a position that pays you.

Spending money on things that are not good for you or serve no good purpose - wasting and disrespecting money ensures that no good will flow back to you.

Giving your money to other people and causes, when you need it more yourself - putting yourself last is giving the same message to the Universe!

Allowing other people to have access to your credit cards or accounts - this is an act of disrespect towards yourself..

Trusting the wrong people when it comes to money - not everyone has your best interests at heart. Not everyone is trustworthy. Having your own best interests at heart is an act of self-love.

Using money for ill-gain or to manipulate or control other people - the use of money for bad intentions or ill-gain will create negative karma for you. This is the Universal Law of Karma. Whatever you do to others, you do to yourself.

Making choices based on greed - the desire to make money without the exchange of positive energy will eventually backfire. Get-rich-quick schemes or investing in something that is not good for people or the planet so as to make as much money as you can will affect you in a negative way karmically.

Not making legal/financial agreements where necessary - having clear intentions backed up by legal and financial agreements where necessary will protect you and your assets. These agreements include legal divorce settlements, pre-nuptial or domestic agreements and legal business agreements.

Not taking care of yourself and your existing assets - if you do not value and take care of all that you have now, you are unlikely to attract more of it into your world. When you take care of yourself and your assets, you are sending a clear message to the Universe that you are worthy of more.

Not saving - if you have no savings, life can feel scary because you have no financial cushioning for if/when you are faced with unplanned expenses. Saving at least ten percent of your income will create a feeling of security and abundance, as well as satisfaction and optimism, as you watch your nest egg grow.

Not having a retirement/superannuation plan - it is wonderful to live in the now, but also wise to plan for the future.

Choosing to be financially illiterate - because there is a lot of "jargon" used in the financial world that is designed to bamboozle, confuse and disempower the average person, it is not unusual to feel a sense of shame and a desire to stick your head in the sand when it comes to understanding financial terms and services. Nowadays, this does not have to be difficult. There are now many websites and books available that clearly explain all you need to know, and it is not necessarily complicated.

Many of these self-sabotaging behaviours are common in the current world population. Unless you take affirmative action, you cannot enter the money matrix. If you have identified with any of these self-sabotaging behaviours, we will be addressing how to put them right in Truth 9.

For now, it is time to declare:

I recognise the actions that do not serve me.

I am willing to release the behaviours that sabotage me.

I no longer wish to sabotage myself financially.

I am willing to do things differently.

I'd like to share with you now how to heal from past mistakes, loss and debt.

Truth Number 8

You can heal from past mistakes, loss and debt

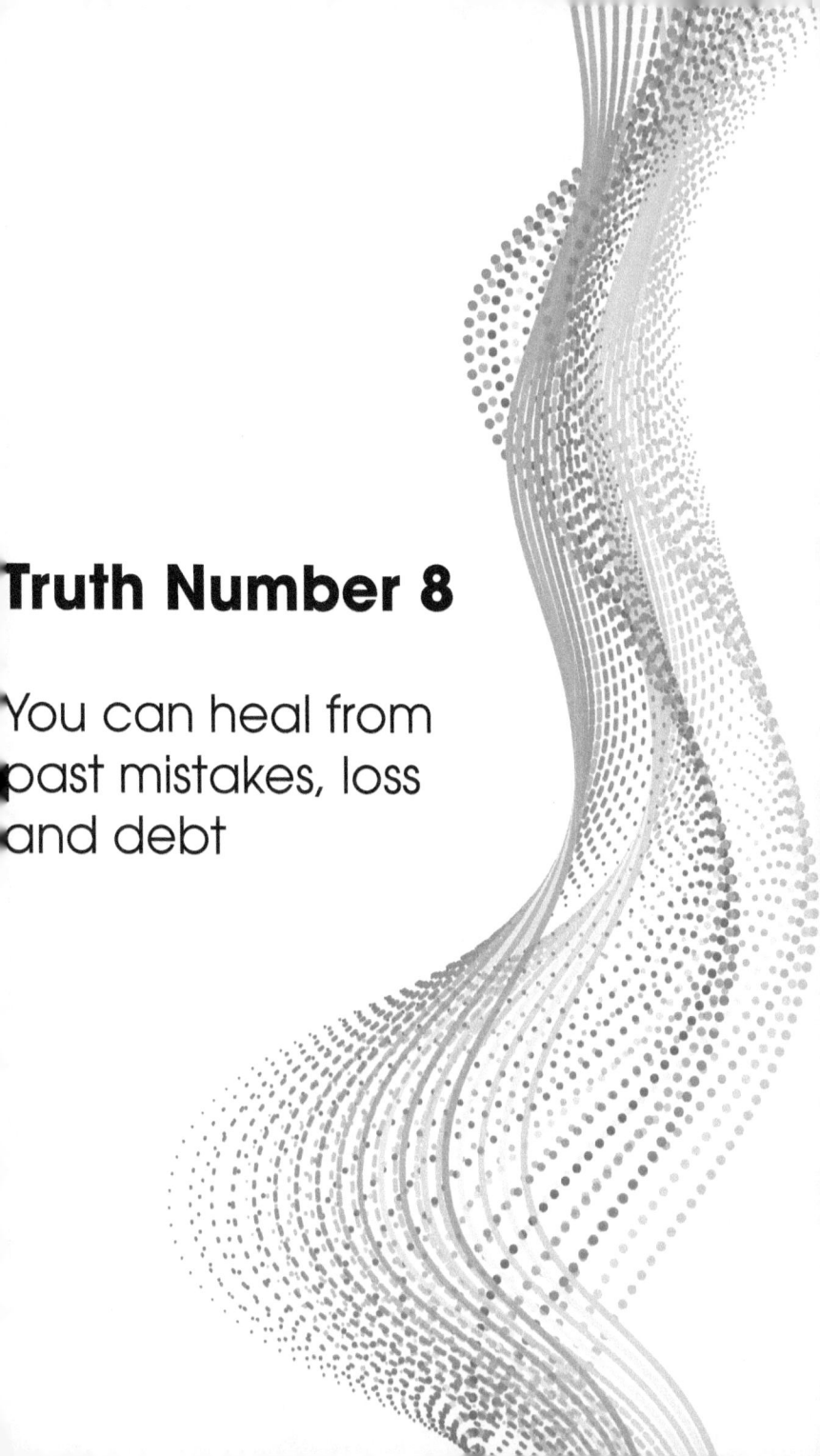

You can heal from past mistakes, loss and debt

Before you can move forward and create wealth-affirming behaviours, it is important to examine your past money story and heal yourself from any trauma or pain. If this goes undone, you are likely to punish or limit yourself unconsciously in the future.

Forgiveness of ourselves is imperative. There are no mistakes, only lessons. Every mistake you have ever made was a decision that felt right at the time, and therefore it was right. You were meant to make the mistake so as to learn a valuable lesson which you can take with you into the future.

Forgiveness of others is also required if you are to live your best life. A loving and open heart is able to receive fully from the Universe; a hardened heart closes itself off to all that the Universe wants us to have.

The Universal Law of Forgiveness deems that when we forgive, we set ourselves free. We free up energy that gets blocked when we hold onto anger, resentment and shame. We can walk away from difficult or negative people, however, if we do not forgive them, we will be presented with a similar person or situation until we learn to forgive.

Forgiveness doesn't mean that we condone what the other person did. It doesn't mean that we have to keep that person in our lives. It does mean however, that we consciously choose to let go of hatred, anger and vengeance so that we can feel light and free and move on with our lives.

The Universal Law of Divine Compensation deems that all losses will be replenished when we choose to learn the lesson from a mistake or challenge and forgive everybody involved, including ourselves. If we resent the situation and do not take responsibility for our part in it, we block Divine Compensation.

To heal from any past mistake, loss or debt, answer the following questions:

- Have I made financial mistakes in the past?

- Do I need to forgive myself or anyone involved in this mistake?

- What did I learn from this mistake?

- Have I experienced financial loss?

- Do I need to forgive myself or anyone involved in this financial loss?

- What did I learn from this loss?

- Do I have debt that is weighing me down?

- Do I need to forgive myself or anyone involved in this debt?

- What have I learned from getting into debt?

I encourage you to journal on these questions and to take your time to reflect and answer them.

Holding onto guilt and shame will weigh you down and prevent you from moving forward. You deserve to feel light, free and optimistic.

So if you are ready to release the past and move forward into your limitless future, declare now:

I forgive myself for my past mistakes.

I forgive myself and others for past losses.

I forgive myself and others for getting into debt.

I am willing to learn the lessons from my past mistakes.

I am willing to learn the lessons from my past losses.

I am willing to learn the lessons from getting into debt.

I am now open and willing to receive my Divine Compensation!

All losses are replenished in Divine and perfect timing.

All debt is paid off in Divine and perfect timing.

Now let us look at creating new wealth-affirming behaviours.

Truth Number 9

You must create wealth-affirming behaviours

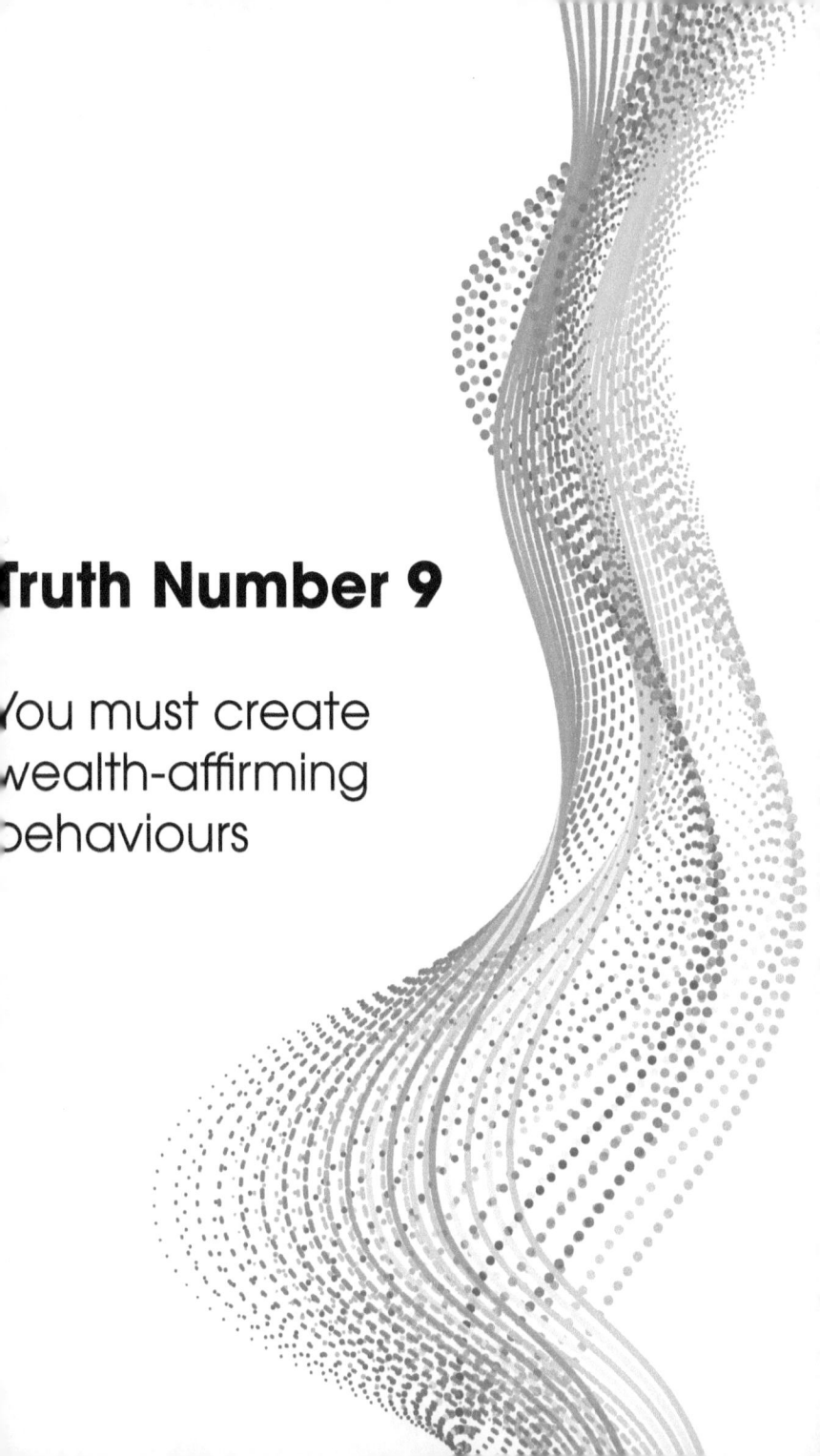

You must create wealth-affirming behaviours

Becoming conscious of self-sabotaging behaviours is necessary before being able to change them. The process of change can be done gradually by taking action on one behaviour at a time.

When that behaviour has been transformed, choose another one, and then another. Make changes at a pace that is comfortable for you, otherwise you could become overwhelmed. Small steps, one after another, are more effective than giant leaps.

The Universal Law of Process deems that there is a process to creating anything. There is a journey to getting anywhere that we want to go. The ego wants to jump from "here" to "there". The ego is impatient and wants everything "now".

The Law of Process encourages us to have patience with our goals and to enjoy the journey of life.

Begin this journey today by owning up to which of the self-sabotaging behaviours in Truth Number 7 are yours and taking action on at least one of them. When you have transformed one, do the next and the next.

Below is a checklist of wealth-affirming behaviours that correlate directly with the self-sabotaging behaviours in Truth Number 7.

Create a financial goal or vision - decide what it is you want. Write it down or create a vision board. Ideally, what would you like your financial picture to be? This does not have to be a complex goal - it can be as simple as "to create $XXXXX per year".

Begin with a goal that is realistic but also optimistic. If you choose a goal that is beyond what you currently think you can have, your subconscious mind may sabotage it.

Assess your current financial situation - in order to get to your goal or vision, you must know your starting point. To assess your net worth, add up the value of all your assets (bank accounts, investments, assets) and your debts. Subtract your debts from your assets and you will know your net worth.

Make a financial plan or budget - creating a basic financial plan or budget makes you more conscious of where your money goes. Make an inventory of all that you spend for a month. Notice what is essential and what is nonessential. If you are living beyond your means or in debt, let go of as many non-essentials as you can. Make a financial plan that ensures that you are living within your means.

Prioritise your spending (wants VS needs) - ensure you cover your basic needs first every month (rent, utility bills, food, petrol etc), and allow yourself to buy some non-essentials only after your basic needs have been covered.

Start living within your means - stick to your financial plan or budget.

Get out of debt - there is both good debt (such as a mortgage or a student loan) and bad debt (credit card debt, hire purchase agreements). If you have good debt, keep up the payments and if you have bad debt, take proactive action to pay it down. There are organisations that can help you. You must be proactive in order to be bad-debt free.

Pay your bills and taxes joyfully - there is a price to pay for anything in life - water, electricity, gas, roads and infrastructure - so rather than resent paying your bills and taxes, feel grateful for having all the modern day conveniences that make life so much easier and more enjoyable. Enjoy paying your bills!

Ask for a pay rise or look for a better paying job / Put your fees up to what you know you are worth - when you take action that affirms your true worth, the Universe rewards you.

Give up working for no pay unless you love it and you can afford it - by all means enjoy your voluntary work if you enjoy it and you don't need the money, but if you do need the money, it's time to get a job that pays you.

Become conscious of your spending - as suggested above, keep an inventory of your spending for a month and notice where your money goes. Then stay mindful of your spending.

Ensure that you are completely taken care of before giving money to others - unless you are feeling at peace with your finances and have everything you need, it is a sin against yourself to give to others before providing for yourself.

Disallow others access to your credit cards or accounts - this is an act of disrespect towards yourself because you are essentially giving your financial power away! And it is not good for the people who are using your credit cards because you are teaching them to be entitled to what is not theirs. This is how you can create healthy financial boundaries with others.

Become aware of where you may have blind faith in others - not everyone has your best interests at heart. Not everyone is trustworthy. Be discerning. Learn to say no!

Use money with good intentions - when you put your money into all that sustains you, others and the planet, the good shall return to you.

Make the necessary legal and financial agreements to protect yourself and your assets - having clear intentions backed up by legal and financial agreements will protect you and your assets. Such agreements include legal divorce settlements, prenuptial agreements, domestic agreements and business agreements.

Take care of yourself and your existing assets - look after your health and wellbeing, your home, your car and anything else that is of value.

Start a savings account - invest at least ten percent of your income and watch your savings grow. You can use this money for emergencies, a holiday or anything else that would enhance your life.

Set up a retirement/superannuation account - contribute regularly.

Get financially literate - There are now many websites and books available that clearly explain all you need to know.

Be kind and patient with yourself as you make the necessary changes that support wealth, and take it one step at a time. There is no need to overwhelm yourself with too much change too soon.

If you are ready to move forward and to correct any past financial behaviour that hasn't served you, declare now:

I am ready and willing to take affirmative financial action.

I make changes one step at a time.

I am kind and patient with myself as I transform my world.

Let me now reveal to you what a healthy relationship with money looks like.

Truth Number 10

You can have a healthy relationship with money

You can have a healthy relationship with money

How you treat money is important if you want to be wealthy and sustain wealth. Just like any healthy relationship, your relationship with money requires:

- Connection
- Good intention
- Respect
- Neutrality
- Giving and receiving
- Appreciation
- Balance

Let me explain each point.

Connection - having a connection to money means that you are aware of its importance. There is no need to "worship" or "idolise" money - that is not healthy in any relationship. And you do not need to deny or diminish its importance either. What is important is that you recognise that money has an important part to play in your life, just like a good friend.

Good intention - money is neutral. It is neither good nor bad, positive nor negative. It is your intentions that determine whether money will ultimately serve you or not. If you use money with good intention, that good will return to you in whatever form you require.

It may be more money, more business, more love, more wellness or whatever it is that is in your highest good. If you spend money on things that are good for you or others - your purpose, your wellness, your loved ones, helping others or to create a better world - the good will return to you.

If your intentions with money are not good for you or others - such as spending money on addictive substances, gambling, buying things that are not in your highest good, investing in industries or things that are destructive or wasting money - the good shall not return to you, and The Source may even begin to close off the channels of abundance. This is the Universal Law of Karma.

Respect - respect requires that you treat money mindfully and wisely, just as you would treat a person you loved mindfully and wisely. Wasting money is an act of disrespect.

Saying "it's ONLY money" are words of disrespect. Respect money and it will respect you. Respecting money means knowing its value and taking the time to manage it and to be conscious of how it is spent. The old saying "A fool and his money are soon parted" is true.

Neutrality - being neutral with money means neither loving money too much nor too little. A neutral relationship with money requires that you aren't overly attached to it and miserly with it; nor are you denying its value. Any healthy friendship thrives when there is no clinging and no pushing away. Neutrality also means that we feel loving and at peace whether money is coming to us or going away from us. You can enjoy receiving money just as much as you can enjoy paying your bills.

Giving and receiving - money is an energy that needs to circulate. That is why it is called currency. The Universal Law of Giving and Receiving deems that whatever you give away returns to you, and sometimes it comes back to you multiplied if you are choosing to spend and invest money on those things that are good for you and for others. Every good human relationship is based on giving and receiving in equal measure, and it is the same with money.

Appreciation - appreciation is gratitude. When you appreciate the money you have now, it will expand. This is the Universal Law of Gratitude. Whatever you are grateful for, you shall receive more of. Whatever you do not appreciate will wither and die. So if you are not grateful for the money you have now, you are unlikely to draw more money to you. If you do not have much money, practise gratitude for the little you have and for all that you have that isn't money too. This will ensure that more money shall come to you.

Balance - The Universal Law of Balance encourages you to seek balance in all things. The middle way is always the best way. When you become extreme in anything, you lose your power. A healthy relationship with money requires a balance of:

- Spending
- Receiving

- Saving.

If you focus too much on any one of these things, you may:

- Spend most of your money and never accrue enough money to invest in a significant purchase like a home

- Hoard most of your money and not create anything significant with it nor enjoy it.

Neither of these scenarios is ideal. When you choose a balanced approach in your financial affairs, you will reap the rewards in every way.

If you are ready to have a healthy relationship with money, declare now:

I choose to have a healthy relationship with money!

I honour the role that money plays in my life.

I use money with good intentions.

I respect money.

I enjoy receiving money and I enjoy spending money.

Whatever I give away returns to me.

I appreciate money.

I seek balance in my relationship with money.

Now, be prepared for miracles... and challenges.

Truth Number 11

Be prepared for miracles and challenges

Be prepared for miracles and challenges

When you make the intention to become financially abundant, you will be met with both positive and negative situations. Both are gifts from the Universe. The positive situations are showing you where you are aligned with the truth, and the negative situations are showing you where more transformation is needed.

As you grow more into your true abundant self, your vibration changes and you will experience and witness money miracles. I have seen and experienced too many money miracles not to know that this is true. Money miracles can come in the form of an unexpected windfall such as a tax refund or a monetary gift, a job or investment opportunity or an idea that creates wealth.

You will also be presented with situations that bring up every self-limiting belief and financial fear. For example, you may experience certain channels of income disappearing, so as to challenge your belief that money comes only from that source, rather than THE Source. This is a reminder that there are many channels of abundance, and that when one door closes, another opens, and perhaps even more than one.

Another example would be a series of unusual expenses, such as car repairs, an emergency plumbing problem, a medical expense or a parking fine. This may bring up deep fear and the belief that you are never going to get ahead, and is simply a manifestation of an old belief that is not fully cleared yet.

Healing your relationship with money is a process. This is because you are transcending very old conditioning that goes back many generations.

The Universal Law of Timing deems that there is perfect timing built into every process. The Universe is in charge of the timing and not you. We live in an ego driven world of enforced timelines and deadlines, which have created a lot of stress. Know that the process to becoming financially empowered already has a divine timing built into it, so relax and allow things to transform and unfold organically.

On the journey of transformation we must face every single fear and every self-limiting belief through our earthly experience. There are no shortcuts to achieving anything of true value. We must transform ourselves deeply and authentically so as to know our true power.

The Law of Challenges deems that problems and challenges are built into everyone's lives because we are all here to transform and to grow, and we transform and grow through being challenged and resolving the challenge.

The Law of Challenges encourages us to embrace our difficulties, for through them, we transform and ascend into a higher version of ourselves and our understanding of life.

In any instance where you are challenged financially, you will likely feel fear. Fear is False Evidence Appearing Real.

Every challenge, hurdle or problem is a reminder to turn to your eternal truth that abundance is your Divine birthright and the condition of your life. It is an opportunity to connect to The Source and to ask to be cleared of everything within you that has created the problem and the fear.

The Universal Law of Healing deems that we have the power to heal ourselves when we ask for healing from the Universe. Sometimes the healing may come as a change of perspective and a feeling of optimism and peace; at other times you may receive an insight and be propelled to take certain action.

Stay aware and know that you are never

alone. You are a part of something greater - The Source - and The Source loves you.

The Universal Law of Surrender deems that whatever is surrendered to the Universe shall be dealt with by that Divine Intelligence which knows exactly how to go about things. Universal Intelligence is well beyond yours, so when you surrender, you shall receive help of the highest order.

The Law of Surrender encourages you to let go and allow the Divine Intelligence to work for you.

So if you are ready to surrender any problems or fears to the Universe, declare now:

I surrender to the Universe my financial challenges.

I surrender to the Universe my fear.

I surrender to the Universe all limiting beliefs I hold about money.

I surrender to the Universe all limiting beliefs I hold about myself.

I am willing to know that the power is within me to be financially abundant.

I am willing to know that abundance is my Divine birthright and the condition of my life.

No matter what the challenges you face, there are 4 keys to staying on the money matrix.

Truth Number 12

There are 4 keys to staying on the money matrix

There are 4 keys to staying on the money matrix

Going forward, there are four keys to staying on the money matrix:

- Intention
- Awareness
- Gratitude
- Faith

Intention - having a clear intention that you wish to live an abundant life rather than having an intention that focuses only on money will serve you in a truly fulfilling way. Focussing on money alone will not necessarily lead to fulfilling outcomes.

Remember that money is the VEHICLE to achieving the abundance you desire - whether it is a beautiful home, travel, experiences, purpose, wellness and things. So it is wise to make your intentions about those things you wish to have, as opposed to just the money.

The Universal Law of Attraction deems that whatever you think about, dream about, talk about or write about, you draw to you. So imagining what you want and feeling like you already have it creates the perfect vibration to bring about its manifestation.

You can utilise this law by creating a vision board that includes pictures of everything you wish to manifest, or you can also use this law by creating a statement about what you want to manifest.

For example *"I am happy living a life of abundance, wellness and purpose"* is a statement you could say every day. This affirmation is taken in by the subconscious mind which will go about creating this new reality.

You can also use the Law of Attraction

to create the money you wish to have by visualising your ideal bank balance or your bills paid. Visualise this until you are feeling that it is real and then give thanks to the Universe in advance.

The Law of Attraction encourages you to trust in the Universe as to the "how". Your job is to visualise and to feel that you already have it.

Awareness - staying aware means that you remain aware of yourself and how you are feeling and all that is happening around you. Awareness requires the ability to observe and to not get caught up in outside dramas. Awareness creates a spaciousness of mind where you no longer live on autopilot, but rather you know that in every moment you have choice as to how you are perceiving any situation and responding to it.

In awareness, you will know whether you are looking through the old filter of lack and limitation or through the new filter of abundance and unlimitedness. When you are aware, you know when you have fallen into an old pattern and operating from an old belief.

The more aware you are, the more able you will be to see opportunities when they are presented to you. Your intuition will become greater and the intuitive path IS the way to abundance.

The best way to become more aware and detached is to create a regular meditation practice. I have included a simple mindfulness practice in the back of this book.

Gratitude - you cannot be on the money matrix without an attitude of gratitude. When you are appreciative of all that you have now, you shall attract more to you.

This is the Law of Gratitude which deems that whatever you feel grateful for, and appreciative of, will expand. When you are in genuine gratitude, you are focusing on what you already have and feeling good about it. From this place you are able to manifest more.

Because of old programming however, we can easily fall into noticing what is lacking in our lives, and what we haven't got. From this place of lack we cannot manifest anything more. Trying to manifest from a vibration of lack is like trying to grow crops in barren soil. It won't happen!

So it is wise to create a proactive practice when it comes to gratitude. Journal on all that you are grateful for daily, or mindfully contemplate all that you have and give thanks for it. By practising gratitude on a daily basis, you can shift your mindset and vibration from lack to abundance.

The Law of Gratitude encourages us to look at and appreciate all that we already have so as to manifest more. You can download a free Gratitude Journal from my website www.nicolebayliss.com.au.

Faith - faith is something that builds over time, and it is bound to happen when you commit to the process of becoming financially abundant. As your circumstances improve and you are shown that you can transcend old beliefs and limitations and you can manifest your desires, more and more you will trust.

There will be times that you will feel trusting of a supportive and loving Universe and times when your faith will be tested. This is normal and must be expected.

To strengthen your faith, keep an evidence journal. Every time a financial problem is resolved, every time you achieve a financial goal or buy something that you wanted, or experience a miracle, write it in your evidence journal. This way, when you fall out of faith, you can look through your evidence journal and remind yourself that you are always supported by a loving Universe that wants you to be abundant.

You can download a free Evidence Journal from my website www.nicolebayliss.com.au

If you are wanting to move forward and stay on the money matrix, declare now:

I intend to live an abundant life.

I choose to stay aware of myself, the world around me and the many opportunities.

I choose to perceive my world through the eyes of abundance and unlimitedness.

I choose to stay grateful each and every day.

I have faith in the process.

I choose to live in the Money Matrix.

Conclusion

You now have everything you need to become financially abundant. Even though this book is not long, the information herein is here to guide you in fulfilling your financial destiny. Self-understanding and acceptance of the Universal Laws are the keys to living in the money matrix.

Be kind to yourself as you allow the truths in this book to transform you, and remember the Universal Laws of Timing and Process - that everything is a process and that every process has its own timing already built into it. There is no need to rush.

Abundance is your Divine birthright. Never forget this. You owe it to yourself and others to grow into your full potential.

And know that as you transform and become financially empowered, you become a wayshower and an inspiration for others. This is how we create a better world.

Love and light,

A Simple Meditation Practice

- Sit in a comfortable position with your back straight, either supported or unsupported, depending on what is comfortable. Some people prefer to sit on the floor cross-legged or in lotus position, while others would prefer a chair, particularly if their hips are stiff.

- Close your eyes and begin to feel the inside of your body, starting with the top of your head and working your way down to your feet. Become aware of the spaciousness inside your body, and notice where you are holding any tension or pain.

- Now allow yourself to become aware of the outside sounds. Listen to them for a minute without judgment.

- Begin to focus on your breath – pay attention to the in-breath and the out-breath for a few minutes.

- Your busy mind will be continually

creating thoughts and feelings, agitation or physical discomfort. At times it may pull you into a fantasy or scenario in your memory, or start making plans for the future.

- Simply override these thoughts, feelings and fantasies by returning your attention to either the outside sounds or your breath.

- Do not try to push thoughts or feelings away. Allow them to be there while focusing your attention back on your breath or the outside sounds.

- Over and over again, you will be pulled into a thought. Whenever you become aware of this, re-focus on your breath or the outside sounds.

- Meet whatever comes up with neutrality and allow the space for it to be there. Observe it and let it go.

- Surrender to the present moment. – over and over again for 20 minutes.

About the Author

Nicole is an author, spiritual teacher and healer who is based in Sydney, Australia.

Nicole works with people all over the world, facilitating personal transformation.

She has written five other books, A Shift to Bliss, 5 Steps to Finding Love, Soul Magic, Soulful & Successful Business and The 25 Universal Laws.

Nicole offers free meditations on the app Insight Timer and her online courses are [available from her website](#).

www.ingramcontent.com/pod-product-compliance
Lightning Source LLC
Chambersburg PA
CBHW020324010526
44107CB00054B/1976